A Year's Lanterns

A Year's Lanterns

A poetic journey through
the darkness of a woman's heart

AURA MIGHTON

Published by Hagalaz Publishing
Canada

Copyright © 2022 by Aura Mighton

All rights reserved. No part of this book may be reproduced in any form or by any electronic or mechanical means, including information storage and retrieval systems, without permission in writing from the publisher, except by reviewers, who may quote brief passages in a review.

Hard cover ISBN 978-1-7782947-2-3
Paperback ISBN 978-1-7782947-0-9
Ebook ISBN 978-1-7782947-1-6

Cover & interior design by Sarah Lahay
Editorial services by Abi Pollokoff

First edition 2022

HAGALAZ PUBLISHING

Contents

Quarter 1: Disappointment & Epiphany — 1

Quarter 2: Exploration & Discovery — 33

Quarter 3: Treading Water & Drinking from Fire Hydrants — 61

Quarter 4: Woman Rising — 83

To all the maidens, mothers, and crones who are waking up

∞

Waking up came to me like a whisper on the wind,
a strange, lulling voice after being filled to the brim
with disappointment—
disappointment, heartbreak, and determination to do
something different.

That voice then yelled at me from the depths
to put pen to paper again.
Forced me to throw a match into the dark abyss of
what I thought I knew of my inner workings, my history,
and my purpose.

Staring into the abyss left me wracked with sobs
and feeling like I was losing my mind.
Choked by words from Old Gods, trees and plants,
ancestors alike;
Flashes of past stories and visions of future paths I had
no idea how to explain.

Until I realized that my words were lanterns in the dark.
Drops of embers, then sparks, then little bonfires telling me to
keep moving forward, while reminding me of where
I had been.

I followed the path of tiny flames through the dark for a year.
The words in this book are the lanterns from that journey,
one of extinguishing old loves, walking through new fires,
and finding nature again.

Perhaps in reading them, you will find your own sparks.
For in this life we are all trying to find our way in the dark,
and the voice that reminds you of who you are—
the one that beckons in the shadows of your heart—
is worth the lighting of a lantern.

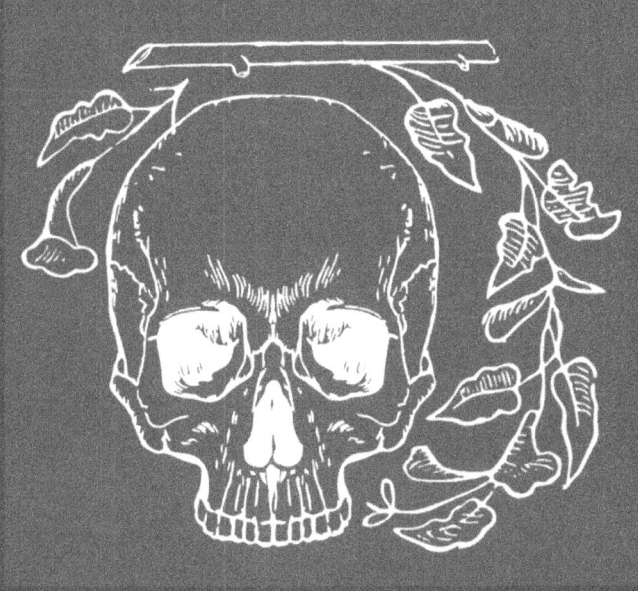

Quarter I:

DISAPPOINTMENT & EPIPHANY

January 20, 2021

There is a passion and kindness that alights new lovers,
but make no mistake:
I am a Venatrix,
not your infinite well of patience and grace.

January 21, 2021

Forgiveness and grace in the face of mordacious words
are touted as the path to enlightenment.
It feels like an unjust punishment as I swallow broken heart
    with tears.
Cruel, but not unusual.

January 22, 2021

I don't want to be the sole lighthouse on the cliff,
your beacon in the dark and only light of safe haven.
I am looking for my mate in lead line,
to be each other's light keeper.
To guard cliff and calm raging sea with equal flame and light,
serving as beacon to each and all surrounding.

January 29, 2021

Hello Moon.
My oldest confidant.
I will shed a flood of tears tonight while you are here,
clear and in full view.
Though you have no words to offer,
I find comfort in your presence,
a haven to share all sorrows
where heaving sobs wash away my broken pieces
from the hidden places your light has found.
All so that I may begin to let them go,
and try anew.

January 30, 2021

Do not try me, infantile man.
My soul may be old and offer visage of cultivated calm,
but I am born of a union of the Northmen;
forebears bred from tempers and axes.
My sun bears the sign of the God of War.
I will eviscerate your existence from my reference,
in the time it takes to pour my scotch.

January 31, 2021

I stand before a full moon,
palms outstretched, feet in the ocean,
and I feel something entrancing.
A calm that washes over me like the waves I stand in.
It raises strength bred from peace deep within.
A strength I will hold at the surface now
to shield my way forward on a path fraught with tempting fires,
now turned embers with Luna's gift.

February 1, 2021

I am "sweet" you say, sir?
Oh hun.
You have slumbered too long and forgotten how to see a woman.
I am the fire in your lungs when you can't breathe after I leave.
I am the ache you feel in the night when your withdrawal ignites.
I am the Moon that commands your tide and will be gone
   in the morn.
Confuse me for candy and you best return to naptime.

February 2, 2021

Woman, hear this,
your ignivomous of words:
Do not have the force to scorch this earth and alter paths
    as you desire.
They are met with the apathy of the sea swallowing arrows of fire.
Hear this: if he wanted to, he would.

February 3, 2021

This carcass was burnt long ago
by flames ablaze from your thousand carelessly tossed matches.
Blinders escorted you past the ashes,
littering the retort that was our home.
How surprising that when someone else found fertile soil in
    the embers,
you thought to reclaim sacred ground.
This succession is not yours to plunder.

February 4, 2021

I am not one for chess.
I prefer swordplay—if I must endure games—
a swift and visceral death for my opponent,
not Machiavellian maneuvers
for Kings and Queens in jest.
The pyre to Valhalla is all the better to toast my scotch.

February 5, 2021

This garden is meant for exploration,
like an uncharted basin or ancient glen
full of delights and dangers.
Pay heed, my handsome friend:
the timid and callous will bear a Goddess's wrath
and expulsion through the gates.
Those of purpose and strength of heart,
may watch orchids bloom
and feel the divinity of Eden.

February 6, 2021

Yes, I am mighty,
some have said formidable,
though I am still lashed by careless words,
though I am bruised by conflicted actions.
Do not believe this heart is walled
because my spirit refuses to darken.
I will claw my way, if needs must.
The mighty continue,
for giving up is insufferable.

February 7, 2021

I am thinking of you this morning.
Your laugh.
Your beard in my hands, temple touched to mine.
The grumble that escapes when you're in the crook of my neck,
hands on the small of my back.
This sensation could be vorfruede,
though the edges of my being whisper otherwise...
Anam Cara.

February 7, 2021

When I cannot have the Moon to draw strength,
I return to the woods.
The aura of the trees is comforting embrace.
Their voices, a slow sway that lulls.
I am ready now.
Beware.

February 8, 2021

You foolish boy,
to have wasted the gift that was love
with your timidity and vacillation.
Now you dare ask forgiveness with a pittance of justifications.
The weak make excuses,
and children do not feast at this table.

February 9, 2021

Oh, my beauties.
I wish to serve as shield for your heart,
to carry the load of all your tears.
Though how could I ever steal your summit,
so as to selfishly keep you on safe ground?
Great love only comes from great lessons.
I concede to serve as Sherpa,
though one with axe and sword for the journey—
I am still a Mother of the North.

February 12, 2021

Return to the woods, my sweets.
The Ancient can be felt where the stillness settles.
Curl into their limbs for rest and comfort.
There is warmth and wonder in the darkness of this winter.
You will find it
when you return to the woods.

February 13, 2021

You manifest in small, unexpected moments.
The ache of you returns with full force
as though we were but a moment ago.
All the things we had and lost.
All the things that could have been
but for fear,
the heartache of consequence,
and lack of words.
The breath is knocked from me again,
and I am left gasping,
waiting for the ebb.
I do mourn the living.

February 14, 2021

Something dark is rising in me,
malefic and nefarious.
Amassing my vices,
the rage of broken promises
and fury bred of misused words.
That which I kept caged for too long is climbing the wall.
The havoc I wreak will be wicked and delicious.

February 14, 2021

The heat within is constant, radiating.
Melting snow beneath bare feet, undaunted.
Warming these sheets, smoldering.
Do not lay hands upon nor draw me near if ill-prepared.
I will not control this fire.
Dance in the flames with me, or burn.
The delight is yours for choosing.

February 23, 2021

Welcome back, my hawk spirit.
How was the hunt?
Yes, I feel your piercing wisdom and vision.
I heed your reminder:
Pay. Attention.
Remember who you are.

March 1, 2021

A curse was thrown on my heart years ago:
"I hope what you have done, someone does to you."
Words thrown for reasons
but without regard for contribution in cause.
Now this iron shackle burns;
I bear its scars and *mágoa*.
I know it will break, one day...
Freedom bred from the fire within me
or by the liberation of a new King.
Right now, it feels long in coming.

March 1, 2021

The Siren is drained and battle weary.
She and the Crone will now share the path ahead,
arms linked, walking toward the end,
though still searching for their champion.
A worn Warrior, with old eyes and heavy axe,
embodying the source of our querencia,
matching the Siren's voracity,
lauding the Crone's manifest.
Lanterns are aflame; her call has been released.

March 2, 2021

The pieces are coming together.
I am telling my own fortune,
I am pulling old gifts from the deep
like blocks of peat from the moors of my mind,
igniting a blaze to gaze within my shadows.
Now I see the name for all this passion, strength, and battle-rage.
A tidal wave of clarity swallows me,
extinguishing any hesitation at the singe of burning hues.
I am rising anew
by the brilliance of Freyja's golden glow.

March 7, 2021

To be devoured by a man's eyes,
bitten along graceful lines,
savage hands, and flicks of pleasure...
This is the comestion between two warrior loves
that has me starving beneath the Moon.

March 8, 2021

I am slowly teaching my daughters the old ways.
Together we unfurl the secrets of our lineage.
They will not endure the shame and scoffing,
the fear of rising gifts with no guide.
In this, I root their foundation:
the wonders of this life are boundless
for those willing to listen and love with open hearts.

March 24, 2021

I have walked within my shadows.
I know the fuel that provokes this woman
to set ablaze the land of her foes.
The pain of lost battles has taught a lesson, though.
It's much more effective to light an insidious candle
    on their hearth,
giving power to the witches within their land,
igniting a controlled burn of revolt.

March 27, 2021

Though the Vanadís speaks to me
and pulls the tapestry of my soul to her altar;
there is no greater moment of bond
than that of the communed spilling of golden tears.
In the name of lost loves,
from this life
and life before
and those not yet lived.

March 28, 2021

When candlelight trance sets my skin to shiver,
I recall when He pulled me to mount.
We would ride the woods,
tresses in the wind,
arms outstretched as in flight,
with the whisper of trees, brilliant sun, His scent a haven.
Reaching the cliff height to look beyond,
my Horned One takes embrace,
tender savagery, balanced.
Now *saudade* is all that remains.

March 30, 2021

Last night, a Raven visited my dreams,
perched before a hearth with blazing fire.
He murdered two wee birds frittering away
on either side of him.
Raven turns and says to me
Get going or I will have that upon you.
His eyes burned red
before calmly turning back to watch the flames,
while Perfection and Minutiae lay dead upon the stones.

Quarter 2:

EXPLORATION & DISCOVERY

April 7, 2021

Sometimes I'd like to step across the forest bridge,
never returning from the other side,
forever lost in the magic of the woods.
The ancestors are quick to remind me:
You can't escape your shadows on this path.
You can only walk through the dark
to reveal the bounty of your growth.

April 8, 2021

Just as I feel I have embraced the Crone—
calm, calculating, and exacting
in manifesting my outcomes—
there is inevitably an event that provokes
the Mother of the North,
unleashing a wrath from beneath my surface
that knows no bounds.

April 10, 2021

Under this dark moon,
in preparation for my new moon solar return,
my gratitude and loyalty
to the Vanadís
for the release of my impediments,
and to the Wanderer
for the thirst of wisdom on this path.
Now, tomorrow's celebration shall be brazen.

April 12, 2021

To drink from the everlasting
is to diminish the joy
of our most precious, finite gift.
One must let go
to earn the honor and pleasure
of standing within Sessrúmnir.

April 13, 2021

Do not take comfort in your standing with me,
for I take no comfort in standing with myself.
The strength of Kenaz and Isa live in these hands.
I have used them to raise the power of Hagalaz before
and will not hesitate to do so again.
Destruction for necessary change
has never scared me.

April 14, 2021

If you climb the path to the rock spirit
and you find her sleeping,
sit quietly in her peaceful wisdom.
For here you need simply to feel
to understand the secrets
of the eternal forest's magic.

April 15, 2021

Dinner is served, my lover.
I will gladly be your queen,
If you will eat the meat
while I eat your heart.

April 20, 2021

The willow and I have something in common,
a shared skill to toast.
Our darker talent
is playing host
to the ones below.

April 21, 2021

As I walk the woods, the tree speaks to me:
Rest upon my arm, love,
and I will care for thee.
Draw comfort and strength
before the path ahead.
Close your eyes.
Hear the voices of the woods awhile.

April 22, 2021

I am carrying a weight today,
a heavy load of choices
that must be made.
Action that must be taken.
I will raise the grace of an athame,
though it will still land like the blade of an axe.
Hesitation has no place, though,
and time will not wait.
We must all spring anew from melting snow.

April 23, 2021

The strength of our efforts and intentions,
the grace and power of our guides,
the timing of our gifts
define the wonder of our path.

May 2, 2021

Sometimes it is good to be reminded,
you are young and small
no matter the age.

May 3, 2021

I've been to the well again.
Flashes of a face revealed beneath a black shroud,
a glistening cover for the Giantess,
a goddess figure, in robes that hold the stars.
Offering of white flower in consideration for ancestral whispers.
Wisdom to be shared in the night
at the base of world's beloved tree.

May 4, 2021

I will feast alone at this table,
rather than entertain bairn;
until such time as the Warrior Love comes to dine—
the One who eats his fear of my tidal energies
as nourishment
before the exploration of my desires.

May 5, 2021

Those that sexualize, vilify, and monsterize
the Goddesses
announce a bumbling blindness
akin to the clattering of chairs,
for the sheer magnitude and power of their specter
commands nothing less than awe and respect.

May 8, 2021

Do you climb below or look through?
Is it adventure or perspective that you seek?
I am the wanderer, and the woods ahead will always beckon
with whispers of wisdom yet to unfold.

May 20, 2021

I will float and watch the fireflies as I wait for you,
for a time and place I do not know,
only feel.
Your being, an ache at the edges of my sight.
A darker shadow in the fog of the Tree's well.

The present time feels of hope
and an itch of frustration.
I can almost breathe you in
before all is lost again.

May 22, 2021

I'm calling the Warrior Love with these fires.
I have lit my walls ablaze.
I have crossed the coals
and wear the scars with pride.
This heat twists and turns a body divine.
Tell me where your flame is.

May 23, 2021

Sometimes, something is better than nothing.
Sometimes, something means settling.
I will not settle.
I will live a life of passion, intent, and purpose.
The Goddesses' gifts call me to make it so.

May 26, 2021

I feel the energy of this storm in my gut.
The power is pooling in my palms.
Now is the time to ignite our changes.
The winds are brewing something new.

June 2, 2021

The beauties are coming,
and I can feel my hopes opening with their petals.
I will fill my lungs each morning
and revel in gratitude.
May Hel receive these white blossoms of offering
and continue to grant me the waking of each day.

June 4, 2021

How amusing.
Your "right" wings and deity
are quickly trivialized
and dismissed
with the mere hint
of an empowered pagan witch in your bed.
This is why you are lost.
Silly boy, Witches are for Warriors.

June 19, 2021

The primal tether unfurls from deep within
with hands cupping cheeks,
temples connected;
you are no longer one, alone.
Breath connects,
ancient energies merge,
and so these souls take flight.
This.
This long-awaited return is what we have found,
if only to be tasted in my dreams.

June 20, 2021

May the midsummer breezes that kiss my face,
that whisper to the trees
and fan these flames,
also carry the flying embers of my wishes
to the tomorrows I seek.

June 21, 2021

With the Moon as my center,
the open Water as the wonder of vast tomorrows,
this Rose for the magic of graceful loves,
and the Sun to heal this soul
shall Litha bear the fruit of all desires.

June 22, 2021

There was a fire in the sky last night.
It lit the magic ablaze,
as though hearing the snap of a match.
Words appeared like flaming arrows in the dark
to ignite the spell I cast.
I will ride the comestion
like a Warrior on the longship.

June 22, 2021

With this cast I know she's heard my call.
She's granted the bid of my need.
So I pay heed to her pull for destruction,
moving forward with clarity, with strength.
I will eviscerate the things that do not serve.
With this cast the hunt begins.

Quarter 3:

TREADING WATER & DRINKING FROM FIRE HYDRANTS

July 1, 2021

There is beauty in juxtaposition,
if you choose to see it.
In roiling clouds that carry faces to come.
In filtered sun that kisses your face like a gentle love.
In trees that dance with subtle grace in rain.
In peace in presence of the now.

July 2, 2021

This morning there looks to be a great Phoenix protecting the Moon,
lovingly looking back while providing shelter,
just like the Warrior Love that rises ever again
to shield his Sorceress.

July 4, 2021

Now is the time.
Sirius and the Sun are aligned.
If you seek peace, ask for it.
If you seek clarity
or love
or purpose,
now is the time to ask.
However,
be honest with your truth,
and be prepared to act.
For in all things,
gift for a gift.

July 5, 2021

I am your Fire Warrior.
Do not come to me expecting a limitless well
of comfort and kind words.
This oracle tells harsh truths,
scrapes at your excuses and procrastination
like a merciless nurse in a burn unit.
You have crossed my path because you are of
the tribe meant to
Change. This. World.
Change needs fire.
It demands Sisu.
So will I.

July 10, 2021

I feed the Light in the day.
Hands in the soil,
sun upon my shoulders.
But in the night,
oh, in the night,
I feed the Dark.
Fan the flames,
let go of things I did not know I carried.
The weight is consumed in fire.
The Goddesses grin in the night,
their smirks curl in the smoke of their oversight.
Tonight we toast the Dark.

August 1, 2021

It has been gray and rainy these last days;
it suits the healing of my Chiron wounds.
The physical world granting me shield,
a soft companion in tears
so that spiritual waters can flow without rebuke.
This morning's liminal vision was pointed, though,
snapped awake with an axe thrown
by myself, to myself.
This time is done.
I must move on.

August 3, 2021

And so it has begun,
born of a feeling I could not explain
from visions that brought me to my knees.
A gentle word from the Owl shook the rocks alive.
Now the force of an earthquake is in motion.

August 15, 2021

The lessons of my shadows are being gifted to my daughters.
The gift is in the wisdom of words,
not of our ancestral slash-and-burn-the-lands.
We will join the wave of witches,
using articulation to transcend our villages.
And so I rest my axe and torch,
in favour of prose and lantern.

August 17, 2021

My hibiscus blooms fall,
curling up to form crimson hearts—
an organ offering for the Underworld Queen.
May this flower float in the Golden Lady's water,
joining the gifts of the Goddesses,
revealing the divine messages of the Hidden and the Sun.
So may two flames find their path to one.

August 21, 2021

I will walk the field of reeds to the river's path,
with dusk setting on the land.
His antler crown casts dark shapes
upon this place of waiting.
For each turn through life's wheel
ends with him in this Shadow Place.
Can we not stay here? My heart aches.
He smiles, forehead touched to mine:
My love,
you cannot live a life in the shadows.

August 22, 2021

With the molting of skin,
we transform and grow.
Or, you can remain bound,
dying on the vine.

August 23, 2021

I collect these crimson hearts
and store them
for the raising of Inguz.
Oh, I shall have what I desire.
Till then,
the bleeding beauties serve
as motivation
during the build to His feast.

August 29, 2021

Storm clouds build,
winds whip my hair,
rain pounds my flesh
yet I am filled with calm.
Every breath I take in the thunder
pools a certainty within my gut:
You must meet the Wisewoman,
the keeper of Sacred Space on the old isle.
She knows what you seek.

September 2, 2021

In wine-soaked candlelight you appear,
seeking pleasures of the skin.
In rebuff, I ask dread questions.
Receive dread answers for my boldness.
Is this divine reality
or the ache of old wounds
taking a twist with salt
before finally healing?

September 3, 2021

In the clear light of morn,
I am no longer torn
by the dread answers.
It's been whispered in my ear instead—
the Trickster God has struck again,
changing shape and stealing forms like only Loki can.
I am all the wiser for it, still.
Bond returned with knowledge in hand,
for, really, only truth was told.
How can I fault a Father
for wanting to help his Daughter—
to ensure Hel's story is told?

September 4, 2021

Weakness does not live in this line.
We fight,
we crawl,
we hang on by single threads.
We batter and bruise,
cry for ourselves,
cry for others,
and then we carry on.
For the path forward is ours to chisel,
and there is no room
nor time
to tread backward on the cliffside.

September 5, 2021

I watched my child swallow fear today.
Sobbing, frozen, panicked fear.
Two platforms apart,
no way to reach her,
my voice and my eyes her only comfort.
All this Mother's ferocity remaining chained within.
I watched her face transform.
I watched the sheer force of will rise in her.
I watched her stand and push ahead with tear-streaked face.
All I thought with a heart full of awe and love:
That's my fucking girl.
We cannot go back. Forward is the only option.

September 10, 2021

I dreamt of stairs falling into the black void.
The numbers of two years were alive and clamoring to pull me in,
pull me back to the way things were and who I was.
I will not do it.
I will not return.
I break my fingernails on the stairs;
I kick and thrash, knocking numbers askew, not caring
    for the mess I've made.
I wake in a sweat; the triple moon hangs in the air:
Hecate with a grin.
Yes, I am certain.
What a ridiculous thing to ask—
the blood on my hands shows how definite.

September 11, 2021

I am inundated with the message of sacrifice.
What to give up,
for what in return,
is murky, elusive, haunting.
I toss the spaces of my mind.
I scribble words until my fingers cramp and eyes are bleary.
What is it you want from me?
I lie gasping on the floor
only to hear a whisper in my ear:
You must give up the love you seek, my dear.
I am wide-eyed and struck by the crystallization.
Now is not the time for hunting my Love.
Now is the time for telling tales and baring my soul.
Only then will old Loves recognize each other in new skin.

September 26

I drank from the fire hydrant until I could stomach no more.
The messages flooded every corner of my being, of my life.
I wrote until I could not think, nor hear, nor feel another drop.
And, oh, how I cried until I was but a deflated vessel.
Now I am floating in a sea of all that I have released.
Unsure of where to go, how even to steer upon these waters.
No matter.
I shall wait here, rocking on the waves.
The Wisewoman of Sacred Space will know the way.

Quarter 4:

WOMAN RISING

October 9, 2021

I knock upon this gate three times,
Threefold, hear my call.
Offerings placed along the lines
of the path to where she lies.

Take me past the greatest tree,
betwixt the fog and shadow.
Dearest Eva, I call to thee:
Show your hallowed stone.

October 10, 2021

In this season of endings,
I'm drawn to the darker thresholds,
to the depths of the woods
where light won't tread
and the voices of the living are silent.

October 11, 2021

The Wisewoman of Sacred Space has spoken.
She has pulled the snag of my every rambling
and masterfully woven the threads with her sight,
a brilliant quilt of guidance crafted for the way forward.
The magic of her weaver's lessons:
Stop questioning the things you know.
This is who you were, and it remains waiting within.
You yourself are a weaver.
Simply visit the door to reveal the loom,
and promise to share the Craft's Arte.

October 12, 2021

When the Gods of Fire turned the dark skies over Gjöll red,
I would not rise to aide either side—
past apathy toward my existence ever-present.
I watched with indifference from the halls of Éljúðnir.
Now all things will come to me.
In time, all things come to Helheim.

October 13, 2021

To all the Wild Women prowling the night,
I share this small insight:
finding your magic begins
in knowing these four things:
1. Believe it to be so without question.
2. Hold space for it in your life.
3. Ask for the help you need.
4. Give the help you can.

October 14, 2021

I see it now.
I see why the ocean and the wind pull my soul.
Where I ground from, with the dirt upon my feet...
My old soul is unfurling,
the door flung wide,
never to be locked again.
I understand the darkness within,
the shroud I wore to hide.
Forgiveness and grace upon my deeds, across all my lives.
And so, I rise,
carried by my own wings,
guided by my own light.

October 15, 2021

How thrilling to come upon
a stone border in the woods,
built long ago by unknown hands.
Is it to keep one out?
Or keep another in?
Only the trees know now.

October 18, 2021

If they want to, they will,
and in the case of either eventuality,
I have equal measure of
ward and beacon
at the door.

October 19, 2021

My heart has been broken more times
than I thought I'd survive,
in tearing chainsaw gashes,
and with subtle paper-cut slices.
Each time I chose to see the lesson
rather than be consumed.
I may be weary, but now I am wise,
and even the oldest tree is loved
by the right woodsman.

October 19, 2021

We all spin yarn in the brightest hues,
weaving for the best possible light.
We do this to darn the tears,
minimize the shameful holes,
mend the broken pieces of our layers.
Remember this, my seamstress:
Mastery of patchwork creates a splendid quilt,
just the same as a funeral shroud.

October 20, 2021

May the Norns look favourably on your day.
May the challenges lead to prosperity.
May abundance be met with gratitude.

October 20, 2021

In this full moon, I say the words.
Hear my humble request.
May they take the flight of birds,
and I shall say no more.
Henceforth every effort on my wyrd.

October 21, 2021

Luna pulls my soul
as though it is the tide.
Every breath I take in her presence
recharges my well of strength.

October 23, 2021

And we shall make one:
despite our differences,
in spite of our challenges,
representing the beauty
of mutually assured survival.

October 24, 2021

Do not cross this threshold
if the watchfulness of a lioness is unnerving,
if the heat of a phoenix is disgruntling,
if the eye of a raven is shriveling,
for all reside within these walls,
keeping hearth and haven
for the steadfast and true of heart.

October 25, 2021

Now this body becomes an offering,
a vessel for the messages.
I no longer fear the dark,
for I command the boundaries.
There is release in this awareness
and peace in the otherworldly union.

October 25, 2021

There is beauty in all things.
The fallen petals are as magical
as the bloom itself.

October 28, 2021

My heart lies in wait,
sleeping peacefully within,
gently lulled by the ripple of water,
caressed by the kiss of this breeze.
One day it shall unfurl
like the blushing petals of this peony.

October 29, 2021

We walk this shadowed, crooked path
to learn the lessons that elude.
The lanterns that you find
are yours alone to flame.
May you reach the terminus aglow,
all the wiser for the next trailhead.

October 30, 2021

Do not heed the beckoning twinkle in the wood.
Mischief lies in faerie light,
and return is not at your command.

October 31, 2021

The approach of Hallow's Eve
brings the scent of death upon the breeze.
Tread warily, my friend,
for darkness may bring your wretched end.

November 2, 2021

Discourse is healthy
and necessary for growth.
It's toxic when only one
or neither party
intends to learn from the discussion.

November 3, 2021

All the versions of my self dance around this bonfire.
Not just the versions I have grown beyond in this life,
but also those that I have lived before, long ago.
We unite around these flames,
accepting each and all.
There is no need to extinguish—
every spark has led me here,
and I need all my torches for the way.

November 4, 2021

To open the door on the black void is a rush of trepidation.
To leap regardless is a lurch of exhilaration.
To learn I could fly is sheer exaltation.

November 5, 2021

Force has no place in commanding the elements.
It is about grace and gratitude,
giving and receiving in equal measure.
You must see the beauty
before you can understand it—
and then humbly request use of it.

November 6, 2021

There is always a beacon, my love.
You just have to be willing to see it.

November 7, 2021

When I close my eyes to travel,
I see how we have fought
Under cover of night.

Völva and Warrior stand shoulder to shoulder.
Determination aligns the force of the elements,
our ancestors and our might.

Our foes fall to the blade
or are lost to the fogs of the land.
Every trace of us vanishing in the black waters of flight.

November 8, 2021

I am coming for you in the dark of your dreams, old love.
Watch me feast on the pieces of your heart.
Those you thought could be excised
as payment in trade for my removal.
Did you not know?
The trade was trick.
Now I haunt your dreams,
and that is so much worse.

November 9, 2021

I have no need of weapons.
The intensity of my raised eyebrow,
the blackness of my eyes,
and the slice of the words from my tongue
are more than enough to remind you
of whom you have crossed
and how you will come undone.

November 10, 2021

Listen to the stripped and howling masts.
Be reminded of why we respect the Water,
And the Winds that whip
dark clouds to block the lookout.

November 11, 2021

By these words,
may the drink in your belly
make real in form
the swine you belie.
Were these the words she spoke?
The spell she cast from clenched jaw
and determined lips?
Her image grabs my gut
and squeezes out Circe's threat:
Oh, I will humor myself by appearing as you desire
—honey sweet, flowing and ripe.
But then, sir,
you shall pay me with all that you have
and rue the day you touched this isle.

November 12, 2021

Some of the memories of our lives—
words said that should not have,
words not said that should have,
actions taken and others missed—
carry wounds that will always ache.
Making peace with them
does not mean forgetting.
It means making a new tapestry
from the weave of scars.

November 14, 2021

May these golden tears
remind you there is a home for you.
May they wake you from the fog of restless travels.

May these golden tears
show you the wanderer's path home
to the love I have kept warm in waiting.

November 15, 2021

I will caress every one of your knots and scars,
for all are beautiful to me
and I wish for no one to be perfect.

November 16, 2021

Sometimes it's a good idea to leave the trail and follow
   the whispers.
You realize there is indeed a path to find,
and the voice you heard saying "no" was just your imagination.
Climb the fence and run the fields, my friends.

November 18, 2021

Hello, Moon.
I live my dreams beneath your glow
and set words to flight
in the draft of your path,
living as if it is so.

November 19, 2021

When a gate to unknown fields opens before you,
may you see the possibility of adventure
instead of fearful trespass.

November 20, 2021

With the light of this blue flame,
I am taken home to you,
to the rocky shores
and forest shadows
where our stories all reside,
in the waters of the other side.

Answers sought
have been received,
so I return to break the surface,
to finish the adventure
only just begun
in the tale His hands have spun.

November 22, 2021

One day, when my time is done,
I will leap from the cliffs and soar.
Through the clouds, beneath the waters,
Returning to the dark, forested shore.

Though now is not that time.
There are stories yet to be told,
scotch yet to be tasted,
and adventures yet to be lived before I'm old.

November 23, 2021

I live as though you are here.
I walk the woods,
looking over my shoulder to see your grin,
the mischief and delight of your eyes.
The wind curls 'round my neck and waist
akin to the glide of your fingertips down my spine.
These flashes inspire my joy
until such that Time sees fit
for me to finally taste your lips.

November 24, 2021

When the winds shifted after this full moon,
I watched the clouds make haste across the sky.
This always signals change is afoot.
I embrace these changes every time because I relish
    transformation.
What I did not anticipate was that the change would be from within.
There is no spell work to be done, divination tool to prepare,
    nor deity to commune.
Instead a current has opened,
as swift as the clouds,
as steadfast as the moon,
and as illuminating as a torch.
So now, I listen
and wait.

November 25, 2021

Centuries of disrespect
for this earth and toward each other
will not be undone in one generation.
What's important is that we keep trying.
Gratitude and perseverance are necessary every day,
not just one day.

November 29, 2021

Lone wonder,
tell me your story
I will sit beneath you,
listening for eternity,
so long as you never stop singing.

November 30, 2021

I am the Siren of your darkest dreams
and the gray Crone of a winter morn.
You must crave both to possess the wonders of my hearth.
In return, I will melt your heart like the snow in my palm.

December 1, 2021

Fear, competition, and insecurity
are like leeches:
temporary things to induce motion and growth,
not to be attached to your soul for any extended duration.

December 2, 2021

If I am still and close my eyes,
the waves carry me away,
and I can see all that is meant to be.
Yet as I return to present shore,
the path from here to future me
is obscured in the Water's sway.
So I am reminded once again
that patience is the order of the day.

December 3, 2021

Of course I value tradition...
insofar as I believe
one must learn the rules
before breaking them.

December 6, 2021

I have been alone for quite some time.
It used to feel like I was trapped,
frozen and drowning
like winter pond leaves.
Now I see there is more peace and clarity
in the dark, watery depths,
and I no longer wish to break the ice.
Now others will have to learn
to sink below
with me.

December 7, 2021

I'm not seeking forgiveness.
Not for this life nor past.
Not from deity nor mortal.
I forgave myself.
I made my peace.
That in itself is feat enough.

December 9, 2021

Climb the fence to touch the creaking house,
but beware the iron wolves.
They roam the grounds,
lurk in shadows,
and hide betwixt the trees.
If you make it back between the Oaks,
the braver you will be.

December 11, 2021

Let this wind and water
steal the breath from your lungs
and every rumble of thought.
Laid bare in the void of silence,
this pause in life before death,
live the guttural truths to *feel*
before words may rise.
Now breathe.
Bring it all to one and remember.
Remember who you have been,
who you are to be.
And now,
you can walk the path ahead.

December 12, 2021

I prefer the searing passion of first touch
to the branding of my heart
or the pyre of its death.

Though I prefer all of these pleasures
to the apathy of never having
been enflamed by love's breath.

December 14, 2021

I am a creature of the dark.
It feeds my soul and comforts this husk.
I welcome Winter in this home with its soothing shroud of night.
All the more time for this witch's mind to take flight.

December 15, 2021

The morning gloom suits for those left.
Weary and weeping.
Grief brings us all to our knees in this life.
Though predictability makes it no less full of strife,
its lashes upon the heart, seeping
until love and time ease the ache.
May the presence of my paltry offering
bring the slightest comfort for the cleft.

December 16, 2021

I have earned the right to be what I am,
to live how I choose.
The question to ask is not
Then what are you now?
The question is
Why did I feel I had to earn the right at all?

December 20, 2021

The point is not how you get there,
how natural,
or right
or longstanding your skills were.
It's that you get there at all.
That you tried.
Then you woke up and tried again.
Anyone dismissing or demeaning those efforts
has forgotten the bravery of trying.

December 22, 2021

I am small, but the trees make me feel mighty.
I am agitated, but the trees make me feel still.
I am loud, but the trees teach me to whisper.
I am lost, but the trees tell me I'm home.

December 23, 2021

You create because.
Not for.
If there is breath left, you must.
Remember this.
In the dark
and in the light.
The shift is inevitable.
Your effort must be constant.

December 30, 2021

Howling winter wind
calls mischief to my mind.
Stirring trouble from deep within,
let flame and cauldron toil begin.
We shall have the outcomes of our desire
by the grace of smoke and fire.
Now bare your flesh beneath Her light;
let them shriek at our cackling flight.

December 31, 2021

I adore the sun on my skin
but my body aches
for the dark
the Moon
and the dance of candles.

January 1, 2022

You dare cross this border.
How foolish to think you would be welcome.
How foolish to think there would be longing and disorder.

There is no flame burning for you in this hall.
The black of my night will swallow your carcass whole.
The black of my night will expunge your gall.

Heed this warning as I lean in.
You best return from whence you came.
You best return before my conjurings begin.

January 2, 2022

There is life beneath the cold.
Not gone, just sleeping.
Waiting to spring forth.
The smallest of nature's creations
understands change and patience.
Why can't we?

January 3, 2022

I walk the winter woods
to collect the crisp threads of thought
that only crystallize in frost.
I weave those threads of clarity into the path ahead.
They shine like lanterns in winter snowfall
so I will never be lost.

January 4, 2022

When every weave of bark
bears the pattern of a gift,
how could you ever
abstain from embracing it?
Gebo

January 5, 2022

You are small and new here, little one.
Sit beside me for a time,
and I will share stories of the Great Turtle.

January 6, 2022

Waterfalls are alluring.
No matter how high nor broad the form,
No matter the rush nor subtly of flow,
I am drawn in like the curve of a shoulder
Or the curl of a grin.

January 7, 2022

I feel the water run upon these rocks,
like your fingertips grazing
the ridges of my spine,
before swirling in the place
between my hips.

January 8, 2022

Let the flames and drum
take you to the dark places within.
A place where the ancient women hum.

The rhythm curls and snakes
Through old memories and secrets.
The ones you keep hidden in the deepest lakes.

Let them rise.
Let them out.
Now is time for you to heterize.

January 9, 2022

Do you ever look upon the stars
and wonder if all the versions of you
are looking up on the other side?
Those past, those yet to be, those in parallel?
If I can travel, they can travel
and we will meet in the liminal.

January 10, 2022

I will send words to flight
like ashes in the wind.
You will return
the long-awaited match
that ignites it all
in flame again.
Feel this flesh burn
as passion's spark
engulfs our worldly bodies
once more.

January 11, 2022

There are those who think I am a demon
and those who call me an angel.
I have played both as needed,
when called for, and in due course.
Such is the nature of humanity.

January 12, 2022

Be gentle in the dark.
When your eyes play tricks,
your mind finds cracks,
and your heart feels heavy.
Slow steps still move forward.
Whispers still hold courage,
and smiles carry light.

January 13, 2022

When you find me,
you will read all the words
I've ever cast
and remember
you were already living here,
in the conjurings
of this witch.

January 14, 2022

It's very clear to me this morning,
the luxury of time is not mine.
The spirits have been waiting patiently for too long,
and there is work to be done.
A basket of breadcrumbs has been gifted to me,
so I am satiated and renewed,
ready to travel again.

January 15, 2022

Two crows cackle from the trees above
while the Moon commands black wax.
I tread lightly today.
Old power is prowling,
and blessings shall unfold as the Gods see fit.

January 16, 2022

Knowledge may be a heavy burden,
but ignorance is wasteful.
There is no bliss in hiding from possibility—
nor fulfillment.
We must seek knowledge until we can no more.

January 17, 2022

Swallow me whole.
Leave me to the dark place,
the land of purple skies,
soft voices,
calm,
and reflection.
The land where I may sink into the water of the stars
and float upon the expanse of my eternal wings.

January 17, 2022

Find me in the woods,
hidden in the safety of the trees,
wrapped in the warmth of moss,
cocooned in a bed of leaves,
like the ladybugs of our Vanadís.

January 18, 2022

It is hard for humans to hold onto the significance of messages
    as time passes,
so the message is repeated at important milestones
until the meaning and purpose become innate
—unquestionable and autonomic.
Only then can the next cycle begin.

In this way, I am being reminded what my purpose is—
not only what my role is but where it has come from and the
    function it serves.
It's not about the end outcome; it really is about the journey
    we must all take

and the contribution of that journey for others.
The freedom in understanding this
is the eradication of doubt and the question "why."
It is so because it is needed.
That is all.

Now you must heed the whispers.
Be strong and start your journey.
You cannot know the path it will take,
but rest assured,
it is important.
It holds weight for us all,
and without it,
the many will be less.

January 20, 2022

Hear me.
Hear me now.
I stand on top of the mountain, screaming.
Screaming like a banshee before death,
like a woman who was sleeping and broken,
a lioness woken up in a fire of rage.
I am screaming as Maiden, Mother, and Crone.

Take your broken heart, your tears, your disappointments,
and bring them to the foot of the mountain.
Your tribe is here waiting.
We do not have all the answers, but we have lanterns.

Some of us have travelled this path before,
we bring a bond of hands and wings,
of love and courage,
to form an unbroken chain through the dark forest.

We move together in this tribe.
No woman is left behind,
until we *ALL* stand on the summit again
to beat this drum together.
To *SCREAM* together.
Wake the Earth,
wake the Old Ones,
wake your Maiden, Mother, and Crone
so never again do they forget
the Power of a Woman.

Acknowledgements

To my mother for believing in me when I thought I was losing my mind.

To my family and friends for supporting me when I woke up and returned to my creative endeavors.

To Emma Griffin of Sacred Space Cornwall for being the Wisewoman I needed. Every woman should visit her while hunting their purpose.

To my English teacher James Howden for showing me that poetry lives in unexpected places, for believing in my voice all those years ago, and for pushing me to submit to my first contest at seventeen. Those words were a marker in time that reminded me of whom I had planned to be when I grew up and jolted me back to life.

www.ingramcontent.com/pod-product-compliance
Lightning Source LLC
Chambersburg PA
CBHW081709100526
44590CB00022B/3707